# Chasing Willow

## A Book About Grief

By: Christina Lynn

# Dedication:

In loving memory of Willow,

Our loyal and cherished companion,

Your paw prints remain forever etched in our hearts.


To Sammy Mozingo,

Your memory is a guided light that forever shines.

In your honor, we find strength and inspiration.


To sweet Ava Elizabeth,

Though your time on Earth was very brief,

Your presence left a profound mark on many hearts.

In your memory, we celebrate the gift of life.


In the company of these cherished souls,

We embark on a journey of love, loss, and healing.

I stare out the window wishing Willow was here. It has only been a few days since I lost her.

I'm so sad.

I can't explain this emptiness I feel.

My mom says Willow will
always be with me.

I don't understand what she means.

How is Willow with me?

My Mom says I'll always have my memories
of Willow.

I try very hard to remember her while looking at the leaves on a tree.

I run fast through the leaves as if Willow is running with me.

I throw sticks into the wind as if she will catch them.

I look at the clouds and see Willow's face staring back at me.

I dream of Willow at night.

I look through my memory

box to keep her close.

Months go by, and my heart
doesn't feel as sad.

My heart seems to grow
stronger every day.

My memories will always be, so I can always
have Willow with me.

My mom and I planted a willow tree to watch it grow.

It's as if Willow is growing with me.

# About the Author:

Christina Lynn is an author with a passion for creating heartwarming and inspirational children's books. Born in the picturesque town of Chapel Hill, NC, she draws inspiration from the beauty of her surroundings and her deep love for animals.

**Author Christina Lynn with Willow and Cassie**

This is Christina's second book, a project that holds a special place in her heart. The book was inspired by a profound and personal experience—the loss of her beloved dog, Willow. Through her storytelling, Christina aims to convey the power of love, healing, and resilience in the face of loss. She hopes that her work will inspire and comfort young readers and their families as they navigate their own journeys through difficult times.

With each page she writes, Christina Lynn strives to bring joy, hope, and valuable life lessons to the children of the world. She believes in the transformative magic of storytelling and its ability to touch the hearts of both young and old alike.

Christina invites you to explore the world of imagination, emotion, and life lessons through her books, and she looks forward to sharing more stories with her readers in the future.